Solomon Wealth Formula

7 Principles To Activating The Wealth Of Solomon In Your Life

By #1 Best Selling Author
Kelly Cole

Publishing Advantage Group
www.publishingadvantagegroup.com

Solomon Wealth Formula
7 Principles To Activating The Wealth Of Solomon In Your Life
www.SolomonWealthFormula.com

ISBN: 0615975828
ISBN-13: 978-0615975825

DEDICATION

I dedicate this book to everyone I have considered a mentor in my life. My dad Pastor Kelly Pete, Both my grandfather's John Pete & the late Oscar Cole, Rodney Johnson, Dr. Oliver T. Reid, Mo Stegall, Matt Bacak, Chris Gardner, Les Brown, Mike Litman, James Malinchak, T.D. Jakes, Jesse Duplantis, Eric Thomas "ET The Hip Hop Preacher, Justin Brooke, Russell Brunson, Aaron Murphy, Michael Jordan, Farrah Gray, Percy Miller, Yanik Silver, Tyler Perry, Oprah, Daymond John, & Barbara Corcoran…If I forgot about you I apologize from the bottom of my heart.

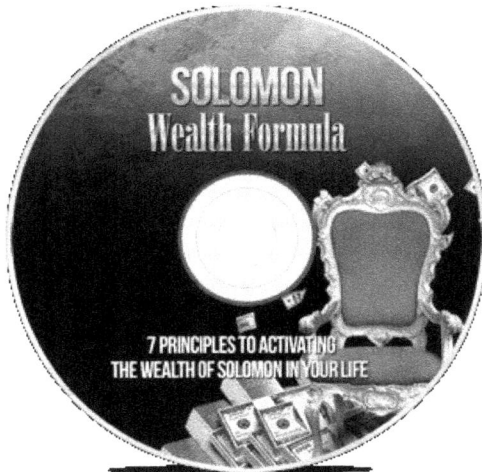

FREE BONUS
Solomon Wealth Formula Audio Training

Be Sure And Download The Audio Training Of This Book FREE Here:
http://www.SolomonWealthFormula.com/FreeGift

FOREWORD

According to biblical standards King Solomon was the wealthiest man in the world, both during and after his lifetime. Yes, you read the previous sentence correctly. *(1Kings 3:5-13)* Try Solomon's financial legacy on for size. Solomon was able to surpass the greats (Theodore Rockefeller, Andrew Carnegie, Henry Ford, Bill Gates, Steve Jobs, and Oprah Winfrey) of our lifetime. Ask yourself a couple of questions. Did Solomon do this without a plan? Was his wealth an accident? Is it impossible to live like Solomon? Was King Solomon's life a fairytale? My friend the answer to all of these questions is *no*.

When you think of that name King Solomon what do you think of? Do you think about the wealth he obtained? Is it prosperity you think of? Is it Solomon's power that comes to mind? Maybe the first thing that pops into your head is the word wisdom, when the name Solomon is mentioned. No matter what comes to mind it is important to note the principles that lie beneath the surface of Solomon's irrevocable success.

Kelly Cole's new book "Solomon Wealth Formula" 7 Principles To Activating The Wealth Of Solomon In Your

Life," strategically maps out the formula to follow to create wealth. Whether you are at the pinnacle of your prosperity, maintaining a standard of mediocrity or at the basement of your poverty, **this** book is for you. Kelly Cole unleashes seven revelatory keys that will unlock and propel the reader into another dimension of Godly Wealth. Prepare to be inspired, equipped and empowered by the resources inaugurated within these pages. To the individuals who are jammed at the crossroads of life's intersection in dire need of Godly Wealth principles to move forward, this book is ordained for you.

"Solomon Wealth Formula: 7 Principles To Activating The Wealth Of Solomon In Your Life" will give you the step-by-step process to live a wealthy life and looks beyond the riches. Discover the formula that allows you to be intentional about building wealth God's way. Discover the blueprints King Solomon used to build his wealth. Fasten your seatbelts as Kelly Cole takes you on a thought-provoking journey that uncovers the secrets of Solomon's financial empire. Prepare to live like Solomon on purpose.

Dr. Oliver T. Reid
The Solution Coach

INTRODUCTION

The revelation I'm about to share with you came to me while I was studying for my Sunday school lesson. I wanted to share some type of inspiration with my students that would motivate them to do something different in the New Year that they had never done before. I wanted them to actually look at their lives and ask themselves, "Am I really living the abundant life God said I could live?"

If they answered no to that question, I asked them why not? Have you buried your talent, have you dismissed your gift God has given you?

While searching my spirit and the word of God for the answer and/or a solution I could share with them the Lord dropped in my spirit Solomon. The scripture that came to mind was 1 Kings 4:34 which reads "And there came of all people to hear the Wisdom of Solomon, from all kings of the earth, which had heard of his wisdom." The reason that scripture came to mind was, I remembered all the people that came to hear Solomon's wisdom, they didn't come empty-handed, instead they brought him a gift of some kind. Now let's relate that to today's time. The people paid Solomon to consult with them on what they needed help with or what they needed an understanding about. So I wrote down to share with my class that one of Solomon's income streams was he did consulting! So I completed my notes and thought I had my lesson together, I would just ask them what specialized knowledge they had, then enlighten them on the fact that they could charge people to consult them.

Just as I was about to close my bible the Lord said read the whole chapter of 1 Kings 4. To my surprise in 1 Kings 4 the Lord showed me exactly what Solomon did to create his wealth, how he did it and how I could apply it to my life. So I want you to read 1 Kings 4 in the next chapter. After you read 1 Kings 4, I will break it down in the chapter to follow. Then I will show you in the following chapters how to activate and apply The Solomon Wealth Formula in your life!

Get ready to start your new life!

CHAPTER 1 - 1 KINGS 4

1 Kings 4

King James Version (KJV)

4 So king Solomon was king over all Israel.

² And these were the princes which he had; Azariah the son of Zadok the priest,

³ Elihoreph and Ahiah, the sons of Shisha, scribes; Jehoshaphat the son of Ahilud, the recorder.

⁴ And Benaiah the son of Jehoiada was over the host: and Zadok and Abiathar were the priests:

⁵ And Azariah the son of Nathan was over the officers: and Zabud the son of Nathan was principal officer, and the king's friend:

⁶ And Ahishar was over the household: and Adoniram the son of Abda was over the tribute.

[7] And Solomon had twelve officers over all Israel, which provided victuals for the king and his household: each man his month in a year made provision.

[8] And these are their names: The son of Hur, in mount Ephraim:

[9] The son of Dekar, in Makaz, and in Shaalbim, and Bethshemesh, and Elonbethhanan:

[10] The son of Hesed, in Aruboth; to him pertained Sochoh, and all the land of Hepher:

[11] The son of Abinadab, in all the region of Dor; which had Taphath the daughter of Solomon to wife:

[12] Baana the son of Ahilud; to him pertained Taanach and Megiddo, and all Bethshean, which is by Zartanah beneath Jezreel, from Bethshean to Abelmeholah, even unto the place that is beyond Jokneam:

[13] The son of Geber, in Ramothgilead; to him pertained the towns of Jair the son of Manasseh, which are in Gilead; to him also pertained the region of Argob, which is in Bashan, threescore great cities with walls and brasen bars:

[14] Ahinadab the son of Iddo had Mahanaim:

[15] Ahimaaz was in Naphtali; he also took Basmath the daughter of Solomon to wife:

[16] Baanah the son of Hushai was in Asher and in Aloth:

[17] Jehoshaphat the son of Paruah, in Issachar:

[18] Shimei the son of Elah, in Benjamin:

[19] Geber the son of Uri was in the country of Gilead, in the country of Sihon king of the Amorites, and of Og king of Bashan; and he was the only officer which was in the land.

[20] Judah and Israel were many, as the sand which is by the sea in multitude, eating and drinking, and making merry.

[21] And Solomon reigned over all kingdoms from the river unto the land of the Philistines, and unto the border of Egypt: they brought presents, and served Solomon all the days of his life.

[22] And Solomon's provision for one day was thirty measures of fine flour, and threescore measures of meal,

²³ Ten fat oxen, and twenty oxen out of the pastures, and an hundred sheep, beside harts, and roebucks, and fallowdeer, and fatted fowl.

²⁴ For he had dominion over all the region on this side the river, from Tiphsah even to Azzah, over all the kings on this side the river: and he had peace on all sides round about him.

²⁵ And Judah and Israel dwelt safely, every man under his vine and under his fig tree, from Dan even to Beersheba, all the days of Solomon.

²⁶ And Solomon had forty thousand stalls of horses for his chariots, and twelve thousand horsemen.

²⁷ And those officers provided victual for king Solomon, and for all that came unto king Solomon's table, every man in his month: they lacked nothing.

²⁸ Barley also and straw for the horses and dromedaries brought they unto the place where the officers were, every man according to his charge.

[29] And God gave Solomon wisdom and understanding exceeding much, and largeness of heart, even as the sand that is on the sea shore.

[30] And Solomon's wisdom excelled the wisdom of all the children of the east country, and all the wisdom of Egypt.

[31] For he was wiser than all men; than Ethan the Ezrahite, and Heman, and Chalcol, and Darda, the sons of Mahol: and his fame was in all nations round about.

[32] And he spake three thousand proverbs: and his songs were a thousand and five.

[33] And he spake of trees, from the cedar tree that is in Lebanon even unto the hyssop that springeth out of the wall: he spake also of beasts, and of fowl, and of creeping things, and of fishes.

[34] And there came of all people to hear the wisdom of Solomon, from all kings of the earth, which had heard of his wisdom.

CHAPTER 2

1 KINGS 4 - KEY SCRIPTURE BREAKDOWNS (WHAT THE LORD SHOWED ME)

1 Kings 4

Verse 1: The Lord showed me first things first, Solomon Ruled as King!

Verse 7: The Lord showed me that the 12 officers Solomon appointed were 12 Passive Income streams, the scripture reads," ***And Solomon had twelve officers over all Israel, which provided victuals for the king and his household: each man his month in a year made provision.***"

12 Income streams that he commanded to bring in income / provision back to his house, 1 for each month! There are 12 months in a year each income stream had a month and King Solomon commanded it to produce income in its month for the King and his household!

Verse 8: The Lord showed me Not only did he command them to do so, HE NAMED THEM – Give your passive income stream Titles

Verse 21: The scripture said that they brought presents and served Solomon all the days of his life – The Lord showed me once you create a passive income stream it is to serve you all the days of your life. (Books, poems, songs etc.)

Verses 22–23: The scripture listed what it took for Solomon's household to run. The Lord showed me I need to think Bigger, expand my mental capacity to live like a King! I'm supposed to have more than enough, a Mansion, "The word says in my Father's house are many Mansions..."(John 14:2) We are not supposed to get the heaven and that be the first time we step foot into a Mansion. We're supposed to be living as heaven on earth! "Thy kingdom come, Thy will be done in earth, as it is in heaven." Matthew 6:10 (KJV)

Verse 24-25: The Lord showed me Solomon Dominated his territory! We are called to dominate the earth, God gave us Dominion! (Genesis 1:26 "And God said, 'Let us make man in our image, after our likeness: and let them have

dominion over the fish of the sea, and over the fowl of the air, and over the cattle, and over all the earth, and over every creeping thing that creepeth upon the earth.'")

Verse 26 – "And Solomon had forty thousand stalls of horses for his chariots, and twelve thousand horsemen…" The Lord showed me those wear his cars, he had 4,000 of the finest cars, Rolls Royce's, Benz, Bugatti – he had them all! With Drivers!

Verses 27–28 "And those officers provided victual for King Solomon, and for all that came unto king Solomon's table, every man in his month: they lacked nothing."

The Lord showed me that they all did their job so much so that everyone who came to Solomon's table lacked nothing!

(Say No More Lack!)

Verses 29-31: Speak of the Great wisdom God gave Solomon!

Verse 32 – "And he spake three thousand proverbs: and his songs were a thousand and five."

The Lord showed me that this was the Overflow – He held nothing back of what God put in him, he released his quotes, songs, poems and books. He spake them! 3,000 proverbs, 3,005 songs!

"Ask yourself, What Am I Sitting On?" What am I not speaking?

Verse 34 – "And there came of all people to hear the wisdom of Solomon, from all kings of the earth, which had heard of his wisdom."

The Lord showed me they did not come empty-handed, verse 21 said"… they brought presents, and served Solomon all the days of his life." Every time they came before Solomon to hear of his wisdom they bought a gift. In today's time that would be called consulting.

Say This Out-Loud, "I Can Consult!"

CHAPTER 3

HOW TO ACTIVATE THE SOLOMON WEALTH FORMULA IN YOUR LIFE

7 Principles to Activating The Solomon Wealth Formula

1– Rule as the King: Realize that God has made you king of your household (V 1)

2 – Command: Realize you have the authority to command as King for things to be done as you commanded. (V 7)

3 – Name your income streams (V 8)

4 – Dominate: God gave us dominion over the earth, you are to dominate it!

5 – Release: It's time to release what God has put inside you so it can produce, that you lack nothing! (V 32)

6 - Live Abundantly: Live the life God called you to live, Abundantly, don't be afraid of what people say about you living the abundant life, LIVE IT! (V 26)

7 – Receive: Receive the increase God has commanded over your life, get comfortable receiving. (V 21)

7 Principles to Activating The Solomon Wealth Formula

 *Rule*

 *Command*

 *Name*

 *Dominate*

 *Release*

 *Live*

 *Receive*

CHAPTER 4

WHAT SOLOMON DID & HOW YOU CAN DO IT?

What did Solomon do?

He created 12 passive income streams that he commanded to produce income for his household, one for each month of the year.

> **Power Of The #12 – Here are some of the biblical meanings of the number 12 to help shed light on why this teaching is so powerful.**

-12 Is a perfect number(referred to by some as the number of perfection), signifying perfection of government, or of governmental perfection. It is found as a multiple in all that has to do with rule.

-The sun which "rules" the day, and the moon and stars which "govern" the night, do so by their passage through the 12 signs of the Zodiac which completes the great circle of the heavens of 360 (12 x 30) degrees or divisions, and thus govern the year.

-12 is the product of 3 (the perfectly Divine and heavenly number) and 4 (the earthly of what is material and organic).

-While seven is composed of 3 added to 4, twelve is 3 multiplied by 4

-12 is the number of organization

-The products denoting production - Products come by the dozen, eggs, T-shirts

-There were 12 patriarchs from (and including) Shem (the son of Noah) to Jacob

-In the New Testament we find the same great principle pervading the Apostolic government as we see in the Patriarchal and National, for we have the following groups of 12:

The 12 Apostles.

The 12 foundations in the heavenly Jerusalem.

The 12 gates.

The 12 pearls.

The 12 angels.

-12 years of age was Jesus when He first appears in public (Luke 2:42)

-12 legions of angels mark the perfection of angelic powers (Matthew 26:53)

-12 is found 187 times total in Scripture

-12 is that it represents divine authority and appointment, as well as governmental foundation and perfection, and shows completeness

-There were 12 sons of Jacob, whose families formed the 12 tribes of Israel with 12 princes; there were also 12 princes of Ishmael.

-The high priest's breastplate, used for judgment, had 12 stones representing the 12 tribes

-The showbread consisted of 12 loaves

-During the period of the judges, 12 judges judged Israel

-*Solomon appointed 12 officers over Israel

-Jesus ordained 12 apostles, who were sent with authority to preach the Gospel and to be witnesses of His resurrection.

-The bride of Christ is pictured with a crown of 12 stars (Revelation 12:1).

How did Solomon do it?

He used his authority as King to command, He exercised his dominion and He released his gifts and talents into the kingdom that they may work for him that he nor his house or anyone that came to his table lacked anything!

How you can do the same?

Just as Solomon did you can create 12 passive income streams and command them to produce income for your household in each month.

Now the 12 income streams can be books, ebooks, songs, poems, websites, a software app and more! It can be whatever God has placed inside you!

Here are some steps to creating your 12 Passive Income Streams!

1. Take out a clean piece of paper.

2. At the top write: What are my gifts? What are my passions? What do I have that will be of value to someone else?

3. List your gifts and passions, if you don't know, pray the Lords reveals them to you.

4. Then write the number 1-12 (a number for each month)

5. Next to each number – write in a passive income stream you are going to create. (Example – Book titles, poems, songs, DVDs, trainings, courses) Many of you God has already given you the title of your book, write it down next to #1.

6. Numbers #2-12 can be different formats of that book that can be an income stream. Example – **2.** Audio book CD, **3.** Audio book downloadable MP3's, **4.** eBook, **5.** DVD from a recording of you teaching what's in your book, **6.** Consulting on the

topic of your book, **7.** Turn book into a workbook, **8.** Turn a Line or key point in your book into a T-shirt, **9.** Enhance your book by simply adding 3 new chapters and re-release it, **10.** Create a conference or workshop around your book **11.** Repurpose your book into different niches that fit. (Example: How to deal with rejection as a teen, as a wife, as a Christian, as an employee etc.) **12.** Do lectures; get speaking engagements from your book topic. (Having a book will brand you as an expert in that field).

7. TAKE ACTION WRITE THE BOOK and Release the book!

8. Release the different income streams!

9. Command them to bring back income into your household.

10. Dominate your niche / passion

11. Receive humbly the fruits from which you shall receive.

12. Rinse and repeat – remember Solomon didn't stop with just commanding the 12 he went on and created 3,000 proverbs and 3,005 songs!

Tips on How to Find Your Passion

Finding your gift or your passion is simple, all you have to do is ask yourself these questions:

What do you love to do?

What is the one thing that you would love to do and just get excited about? You wouldn't have to get paid but you love it so much you would do it for free.

What is something that people regularly compliment you on?

A lot of times our gift or passion is hidden. We don't know we have it or we don't believe that it is a gift because it comes so easily to us but people compliment us on it daily. I would pay closest attention to this, what your answer is to this question, because often enough this is your unique gift or that thing that is going to produce your passive income.

Now it should be easy to you, it should be effortless to you. What I'm doing right now sharing this information with you is effortlessly to me. I love to share information about creating products and using your gift to make passive income. If you put me in a room I could talk about this stuff all day long, sharing information about creating passive income. I remember when I went to my first millionaire's conference; I didn't want to leave. It was in Atlanta, those three days of that conference I didn't eat lunch. I couldn't wait to wake up the next morning to go for another eight hours. If they would have asked me and it was a 24 hour a day workshop, I would have stayed all day and all night without eating and sleeping. I just really love this. I can't wait to wake up in the morning so I can get to work on what I love to do. So find whatever it is that causes you to feel that way and that's your gift, that's your passion.

Quote

"The starting point of all achievement is desire."

Napoleon Hill

<u>The Keys to Success</u>

1. Develop a definite and a clear-cut goal/aim.

2. Draw up a wise workable plan/program.

3. Guard your health. Without health there is no real wealth.

4. You must conserve your energy.

5. Be honest in your life (in words, deeds, thoughts and actions).

6. Stick to virtues and adopt good principles.

7. Reflect upon ideal personalities and seek strength from their philosophy.

8. Seek divine guidance and be truthful.

9. Endeavor to help and serve others with gratitude.

10. Always think positive and believe in the power of God.

Transformative thinking is indeed the way to success. Set out a plan to achieve your goal and deliberately ruminate over the meaning of this plan and make it happen.

Great people from all walks of life have emerged as true victors and the reason behind this is training the mind for happiness.

Ethical discipline is essential, particularly self-discipline.

Each individual is unique. What is good for person A may not be suitable for person B. However, it has to be emphasized that all can enjoy quietude, solitude and silence, and to be honest every individual irrespective of age, caste, creed, color, sex has at some stage or another experienced peace.

After discovering through trial and error method, you can determine the precise way to compose your mind body complex and thus attain great heights.

Be systematic, and your only goal should be to employ methods that bring you success and happiness.

Our mental faculties determine our actions, and it is quite obvious that the mind should be tamed and subdued. Constant vigilance is necessary and continuous training of the mind will pave the path to ultimate success.

Do not fall prey to the dictates of your mind!

Optimistic, heroic and noble ideals have a powerful and uplifting effect upon the body. Enthusiasm with deliberate well-orchestrated self-application in joyous mood and absolute optimism is the secret path to wealth for all great men.

Affirmation for success:

I will pursue relentlessly, as it is my birthright to be successful. I am powerful and I shall achieve what I need at the time I need. I am destined to reap the fruits of my actions and I will share my joy in success with all I know.

Benefits of Affirmations

• Self-esteem and a positive outlook

• Helps you achieve goals and targets

• Improve you memory and skills

• Helps to create an inner self-belief (willpower, confidence and character)

• It can help you evolve spiritually

Words that are spoken will be attractive and procure instant admiration. Wealth is in itself a word, and by itself it does not mean anything.

The one single factor, which gives the word wealth, the meaning is the intellect. The wealth of information is nowhere to be found, but it is within us at all times. Intellect is cultivated through logic, and the main point is that dry logic and philosophy can often prove counterproductive. Thus, it is essential to communicate effectively, because in pursuit of wealth, you will need to sell yourself your business or your company via communication (words).

CHAPTER 5

GOOD SUCCESS

JOSHUA 1: 8

Joshua chapter 1 verse 8 says: "[8] This book of the law shall not depart out of thy mouth; but thou shalt meditate therein day and night, that thou mayest observe to do according to all that is written therein: for then thou shalt make thy way prosperous, and then thou shalt have good success." (KJV)

There are **three** things God told Joshua to do.

Okay the first thing He told Joshua in the scripture was to speak it, He said the book of the law shall not depart out of thine mouth. **Speak it**, which backs up what Solomon done first he spoke, he commanded the 12 officers to do their job and make provision for his household in their appointed month.

Here are a list of scriptures to Speak over your life daily:

Deuteronomy 8:18(KJV)
But thou shalt remember the Lord thy God: for it is he that giveth thee power to get wealth, that he may establish his covenant which he sware unto thy fathers, as it is this day.

Deuteronomy 28:13 (KJV)
[13] And the Lord shall make thee the head, and not the tail; and thou shalt be above only, and thou shalt not be beneath; if that thou hearken unto the commandments of the Lord thy God, which I command thee this day, to observe and to do them:

John 10:10(KJV) …I am come that they might have **life**, and that they might have it **more abundantly**.

3 John 1:2(KJV) - Beloved, I wish above all things that thou mayest prosper and be in health, even as thy soul prospereth.

Philippians 4:19(KJV) - But my God shall supply all your need according to his riches in glory by Christ Jesus.

Nehemiah 2:20(KJV) - Then answered I them, and said unto them, The God of heaven, he will prosper us;

2 Corinthians 9:8(KJV) - And God is able to make all grace abound toward you; that ye, always having all sufficiency in all things, may abound to every good work:

Ecclesiastes 7:14(KJV) - In the day of prosperity be joyful...

Proverbs 13:22 (KJV)

A good *man* leaveth an inheritance to his children's children: and the wealth of the sinner *is* laid up for the just.

Ecclesiastes 5:19 (KJV)

Every man also to whom God hath given riches and wealth, and hath given him power to eat thereof, and to take his portion, and to rejoice in his labour; this *is* the gift of God.

Ecclesiastes 10:19 (KJV)

A feast is made for laughter, and wine maketh merry: but money answereth all *things*.

The second thing He told Joshua to do was to meditate.

Now what was Joshua to meditate on? He was to meditate: what God had spoken to him threw the book of the law. He was to meditate on the word that he had just spoken. As you release your gifts to produce income for you meditate on what you have spoken over them. Also meditate on what God said about you and the power he has given you on earth.

<u>Scriptures to **meditate on:**</u>

Deuteronomy 8:18(KJV)

But thou shalt remember the Lord thy God: for it is he that giveth thee power to get wealth, that he may establish his covenant which he sware unto thy fathers, as it is this day.

Deuteronomy 28:13 (KJV)

[13] And the Lord shall make thee the head, and not the tail; and thou shalt be above only, and thou shalt not be beneath; if that thou hearken unto the commandments of the Lord thy God, which I command thee this day, to observe and to do them:

John 10:10(KJV) …I am come that they might have **life**, and that they might have it **more abundantly**.

3 John 1:2(KJV) - Beloved, I wish above all things that thou mayest prosper and be in health, even as thy soul prospereth.

Philippians 4:19(KJV) - But my God shall supply all your need according to his riches in glory by Christ Jesus.

Nehemiah 2:20(KJV) - Then answered I them, and said unto them, The God of heaven, he will prosper us;

2 Corinthians 9:8(KJV) - And God is able to make all grace abound toward you; that ye, always having all sufficiency in all things, may abound to every good work:

Ecclesiastes 7:14(KJV) - In the day of prosperity be joyful...

Proverbs 13:22 (KJV)

A good *man* leaveth an inheritance to his children's children: and the wealth of the sinner *is* laid up for the just.

Ecclesiastes 5:19 (KJV)

Every man also to whom God hath given riches and wealth, and hath given him power to eat thereof, and to take his portion, and to rejoice in his labour; this *is* the gift of God.

Ecclesiastes 10:19 (KJV)

A feast is made for laughter, and wine maketh merry: but money answereth all *things*.

Now the last thing God told Joshua to do was to Do It, Do what he just spoke and meditated on it.

Just as we discussed earlier, it is very important that we speak! Speak with authority, command things to happen.

And then we actually have to put in the work and DO WHAT GOD SAID WE CAN DO!

Question: Why did God repeatedly tell Joshua to be strong and of good courage?

Joshua 1:9(KJV) - Have not I commanded thee? Be strong and of a good courage; be not afraid, neither be thou dismayed: for the LORD thy God is with thee whithersoever thou goest.

Answer: Because when you decide TO DO IT and Take Action, you will automatically receive resistance.

It's going to come from your friends, your family members, and your church family. Don't be surprised it's going to come from everywhere.

Just remain focused and do what God has put in you to do. Also read this scripture daily, it will strengthen you: Joshua 1:9(KJV) - Have not I commanded thee? Be strong and of a good courage; be not afraid, neither be thou dismayed: for the LORD thy God [is] with thee whithersoever thou goest.

In the next chapter I'm going to give you some insight, some tools, resources and steps on how to DO IT!

I'm going to share with you how to complete the Solomon Wealth Formula Action Steps in the example I gave on how to take your book and turn it into 12 streams of income.

CHAPTER 6

HOW TO COMPLETE THE 12 ACTION STEPS OF THE SOLOMON WEALTH FORMULA

Action Step 1. How to get your book done fast!

Choose Topic / Title

Write an Outline – Include chapter titles and be very detailed about what you want to cover.

To get some ideas of what to write about on your topic, you can survey your audience; ask them what questions they have about your topic. Maybe do a Facebook post, or create a free survey and a website call www.SurveyMonkey.com.

 Then research your topic – make notes of any sources you receive information from.

- Start writing - Fill in the chapters

- Proofread to see if you would like to add anything

- Copyright book – go to Copyright.gov for $35 you can do an electric file copyright on your book.

- Then send your book to an editor to be edited.

- After you receive your book back from the editor review the edits and make sure you approve of them.

- Get your book formatted for the correct book size. Standard book size format is 6x9.

- Get your cover designed – write a clear description of what you want and send it to a graphic designer.

- Decide how you are going to publish it and who you are going to go with.

I recommend you go with publishingforpastors.com we will do complete editing, formatting, cover design & publishing – to Amazon & more.

- Choose Publisher & send them your manuscript

- Set Launch date

- Roll-out Marketing Campaign

- Launch Book

- Continue Pushing after book has been launched

Here are what I call **Generator Shortcuts** on How to get your **book done fast!**

Get 15 Sheets Of Paper

Page 1 Write Title

Page 2 Write Numbers 1-10 down left side, then write the chapter title next to each line.

1. Write Chapter Title

2. Chapter Title

3. Chapter Title

4. Chapter Title

5. Chapter Title

6. Chapter Title

7. Chapter Title

8. Chapter Title

9. Chapter Title

10. Chapter Title

Page 3 Write chapter title at top then 10 questions someone would have about that chapter title.

- Chapter Title

- Question 1

- 2

- 3

- 4

- 5-10

Do The Same For Pages 4-12 Write chapter title at top then 10 questions someone would have about that chapter title.

- Chapter Title

- Question 1

- 2

- 3

- 4

- 5-10

Last 3 Pages

- 13 – Write your Dedication & Acknowledgments

- 14 – Your Bio

- 15 – Write any sources you may have

Then have someone interview you asking you the questions.

- Record on Freeconferencing.com

- They will send you an MP3 after the call FREE

- Then have the audio transcribed by PubforPastors.com ($50 for 60min)

- Then have the transcribed document edited & formatted!

- And Bam You Have A Book!

You can also record yourself answering the questions

- Record with Audacity (audacity.sourceforge.net)

- Export recording as MP3

- Have the audio transcribed

- Have transcribed document edited & formatted

- Bam You Have a Book!

Bonus Tip$$$

Have You Done Public Speaking or a Lecture of any kind?

Video Record your Lecture and extract the audio have it transcribed and turn it into a book!

Ideas

• Put on your own event, video record it, extract the audio, have it transcribed and turn it into a book!

• Home presentation (Invite over family and friends put on your presentation) video record it, extract the audio, have it transcribed and turn it into a book!

• Sunday School Lessons (If you create your own) video record it, extract the audio, have it transcribed and turn it into a book!

• Pastors with Sermons – video record it, extract the audio, have it transcribed and turn it into a book! Every Sunday!

<u>Action Step 2. Audio book CD</u> – If you had someone interview you or you recorded yourself answering the questions you wrote out, you have your audio book done. Also if you spoke your book during a lecture or presentation that was recorded your audio book is done.

Resources:

- Kunaki.com – Package, Print & Ship your CD on-demand Retail ready for $1.00 plus shipping
- Sell your cd on amazon, ebay, your website, events /speaking engagements.
- Create a CD of the month club where you create a new CD every month and charge subscribers a monthly fee to receive them. Example $20 month x 200 people = $4000 a month!

<u>Action Step 3. Audio book downloadable MP3's</u>

Take the CD and Create MP3's

If you had someone interview you or you recorded yourself answering the questions you wrote out, you have your audio book done. Also if you spoke your book during a lecture or presentation that was recorded your MP3 audio book is done.

Resources:

- CDBaby.com – Will distribute your audio book on MP3 to:

- Itunes

- Google Play

- Spotify

- Amazon Mp3

- Zune Store

- Rhapsody

- eMusic

- Myspace

- Nokia

- Tradebit

- Myxer

- And Your Website (They will give u a widget for easy download from your website.)

Action Step 4. Create an eBook

With your book done it's not hard at all to turn it into an eBook. Just use the same files, including the cover and word document.

For Amazon Kindle go to kdp.amazon.com & follow the steps in setting up your account and uploading your book.

For other eBook publishing channels use a site called Smashwords.com where they will distribute your eBook to:

- Nook

- i-books

- Kobo

- Sony Ereader

- Google books

Action Step 5. Create a DVD from a recording of you teaching what's in your book!

Record every time you speak or do any type of presentation, because it can be turned into a DVD that you can sell! Even if you don't sell it, it can be used as promotional videos you can upload to YouTube.

Ideas

- Put on your own event

- Home presentation (Invite over family and friends put on your presentation)

- Pastors with Sermons – Every Sunday

Resources:

- Kunaki.com – Package, Print & Ship your DVD on-demand Retail ready for $1.00 plus shipping

- Sell your DVD on Amazon, eBay, your website, events /speaking engagements.

- Create a DVD of the month club where you create a new DVD every month and charge subscribers a monthly fee to receive them. Example $20 month x 200 people = $4000 a month!

Action Step 6. Consulting on the topic of your book

Writing and publishing a book will automatically brand you as an expert in that field. All you need to do next is decide how much your time is worth, then promote yourself as a consultant.

How I determined my pricing, my millionaire mentor told me if I want to be a millionaire my time was worth at least $500 an hour no less.

Action Step 7. Turn your book into a workbook

To turn your book into a workbook you will need to single out parts of your book that you can add assignments for your reader to do.

Example: In the space provided below write out your list of goals you have for 2014.

In the space provided below write a list of your last 10 sermons.

You could also break down different points in your book and have the reader write down their thoughts.

You could leave a couple of blank pages to have them create a vision board or paste pictures of what will keep them motivated.

Then just like the regular book you can send the Word document to PublishingforPastors.com and they will get it ready and publish it for you.

Action Step 8. Turn a Line or key point in your book into a T-shirt

By far I would say this one is my favorite. To do this all you need to do is choose your best quote from your book. Then go to one of the following resources below sign up for a free account, then create a design and they will print and ship your T-shirts On-Demand.

Resources:

Spreadshirt.com – Print On-demand T-shirt website, you can design right on their site, set your price and create a page to sell your T-shirts.

Cafepress.com – Print On-demand T-shirt website, you can upload your design on their site, set your price and create a page to sell your T-shirts. On cafepress.com you can also create other products like coffee mugs, clocks & more!

Teespring.com – Now Teespring is a little different. With Teespring you can design a T-Shirt on their website, the only thing is you have to set a goal on how many t-shirts you would like to sell and you are given a time frame to do so up to about two weeks. Now if you do not reach your goal, your customers will not be charged and the t-shirts will not print which means you will not make any money. The cool thing about this is you get to test the market and see if your design will actually sell.

Action Step 9. Enhance your book, add 3 new chapters and re-release it.

To accomplish this all you need to do is either write three new bonus chapters or have three experts in your field submit a chapter each. This will allow you to re-release your book as an Enhance or Deluxe copy of your book.

Action Step 10. Create a conference or workshop around your book.

To create a conference or workshop from your book you will need to complete the following steps:

- Choose a Creative Title – example "The Solomon Wealth Conference"
- Create Your Team – Who's going to handle Registration, Administration duties, and Media debt?
- Choose a date
- Find a venue – Make sure the venue has everything you need. Check the size, do they have a projector, tables, chairs, refreshments etc.
- Contact and confirm your speakers (If you are not going to be the only one)
- Set Registration price or make it Free
- Setup Eventbrite for online ticket registration if you are charging for registration.

- Sponsor Request Form – This is a form that lists the benefits of your event that you can send to a potential sponsors requesting them to sponsor your event.
- Vendor Request Form – This form is what you would send out to companies or vendors that fit the theme of your conference, so they can set up a table to sell their product or services.
- Event Schedule / Plan – Your plan needs to be a very detailed minute-by-minute plan of what's going to happen when & where at your event.
- Setup a conference landing page – collect names and emails, build a database to market future events and products. (A great place to get a free sign-up form is Mailchimp.com)
- Get your event flyer designed
- Start Your Marketing Campaign – Create a Facebook Event, Create a promotional Video explaining who, what, when & where, Create a Craigslist event ad, Email your list of subscribers, if you have any.
- Hire Videographer to Record Whole Event – So you can sell The DVDs online
- Hire Photographer
- Finalize all plans
- Put on a great event

Action Step 11. Repurpose your book into different niches that fit.

Another great way to create multiple streams of income from your book is to repurpose it for different niches. Example: How to deal with rejection as a teen, as a wife, as a Christian, as an employee etc.

All you need to do is maybe edit the content a little by adding the keyword to the book so it reads for someone dealing with rejection as a teen, wife or whatever.

Then just follow the same steps as you did with the first version and republish it.

The best example of this is the "Chicken Soup for the Soul" book series.

Action Step 12. Do lectures; get speaking engagements from your book topic.

Just as I mentioned earlier having a book will brand you as an expert in that field.

And being viewed as an expert will land you speaking engagements. Below are some ways to get speaking engagements and a few marketing ideas.

- Create a speaking promo video, announcing that you are available for speaking engagements.

- Create a speaker flyer / one sheet with picture, short bio, book title, awards, credentials if any, testimonials if any, speech topics, list or logos of places you spoke.
- Post Craigslist ads daily in the event services section
- Post videos regularly on YouTube, create a weekly segment or show
- Do online classes – Teleseminars, Webinars, Live Streams
- Use social media to create the following – Facebook Fan Page, Twitter (Tweet quote from your book or topic), Linkedin
- Ask yourself "Who do I know, and who knows, who I need to know?" Ask that person to connect you to someone that could book you to speak or do a lecture, at Colleges, Churches, Organizations, Clubs & Groups.

Those are 12 things you can do to turn your book into 12 income streams, one for each month.

Review:

1. Write & Publish Your Book
2. Create Audio book on CD
3. Create Audio book as MP3's
4. Publish as eBook
5. Release A DVD
6. Start Consulting
7. Turn your book into a workbook
8. Create a T-shirt
9. Enhance your book add 3 new chapters and re-release it,
10. Create a Conference
11. Repurpose your book into different niches that fit.
12. Do lectures; get speaking engagements

Remember the first step is to TAKE ACTION, WRITE THE BOOK, GET IT PUBLISHED.

My Goal for this year is to release a book every month that I command to provide provision for my household, one for each month.

Just like Solomon I'm not going to stop there I'm also going to turn each book into an ebook, an audio book and a DVD.

CHAPTER 7

BONUS IDEAS TO CREATE PASSIVE INCOME

Camtasia Video Training Videos – This strategy will work if you have training or a specialized knowledge you can teach on your computer. Camtasia is software that will record video and audio of whatever you are doing on your computer screen. This is great for anything you can teach step-by-step. Examples how to build a website, how to search Google for answers, how to use Facebook.

Use can order Camtasia at: www.techsmith.com/camtasia

There is a Free Version called Camstudio you can get: www.camstudio.org

A great place to sell your training course is a website called **Udemy.com**. Udemy is a huge online training website where people come to learn different things, from Cake decorating to how to improve your golf swing!

Examples:

849 Students x $49 = $41,601

2936 Students x $99 = $290,664

As you can see uploading a training course to Udemy could be very profitable for you.

<u>Interview Experts In Any Field</u> - Interview Experts in any field and create Kindle ebooks.

Here is where you can find experts to interview:

- RTIR.com

- Facebook

- Twitter

- Family, Friends, Neighbors

- Anybody with specialized knowledge is an expert

What to Do Next:

- Contact the expert – say something like, Hello, I am writing a book about ____and I would love to interview you and include you on my panel of experts.

- Schedule a time

- Sign-up for a free conference line at FreeConferencing.com

- Send them the number and pin to call

- Record The Interview

- Have the MP3 transcribed

- Get the transcribed document edited and formatted

- Get a cover created

- Upload it to Amazon Kindle Marketplace

- Kdp.amazon.com (Sign up Free Account)

The Great thing about this strategy is when you are done, you will have an audio you can turn into a CD to sell online, plus the ebook!

Compilation books – This idea is not a new one, but I think people forget about it. Choose a topic or a niche and have people submit their stories to be included in your book. I have seen this done two different ways. For starters I seen people charge a fee to submit a story and have it placed in the book. The second way I have seen is the author allows people to submit stories for free and charge the contributors on the backend a wholesale cost to purchase books. Either way you choose will work out just fine.

<u>Create Simple Children's Books For Kindle</u> – Creating children's books for Amazon kindle is very easy to do just follow these simple steps.

- Find easy subjects that children like – Dinosaurs, Butterflies, Solar System.
- Educational, Non-Fiction & Interesting topics for kids only 700-800 words
- Use Wikipedia for research Use Wikipedia for research (You must write in your own words)
- Use short sentences / short text blocks
- Use a lot of public domain images (Search.Creativecommons.org)

CHAPTER 8

ARE YOU BURYING YOUR TALENT?

"The gift, talent or ability God gave you is your key to success. He did not give it to you to waste He gave it to be used and invested." ~ **T.D. Jakes Ministries**

We have all been given something from God, a special talent, gift or ability, something that comes easy to us but harder to others.

The problem is because we don't believe in our gifts, talents and abilities we end up burying them and working at jobs we hate and for bosses who don't care about us or our family.

It's easier to bury your talent than to put in the work and let it produce the kind of life we deserve and desire, the life God said we can live.

So I ask you, "Are you burying your talent?"

If so, I command you right now to dig it up and get to work. Don't be like the wicked servant in the scripture below, allow your talent to produce for you.

Matthew 25:15-18

[14] For the kingdom of heaven is as a man travelling into a far country, who called his own servants, and delivered unto them his goods.

[15] And unto one he gave five talents, to another two, and to another one; to every man according to his several ability; and straightway took his journey.

[16] Then he that had received the five talents went and traded with the same, and made them other five talents.

[17] And likewise he that had received two, he also gained other two.

[18] But he that had received one went and digged in the earth, and hid his lord's money.

[19] After a long time the lord of those servants cometh, and reckoneth with them.

[20] And so he that had received five talents came and brought other five talents, saying, Lord, thou deliveredst unto me five talents: behold, I have gained beside them five talents more.

²¹ His lord said unto him, Well done, thou good and faithful servant: thou hast been faithful over a few things, I will make thee ruler over many things: enter thou into the joy of thy lord.

²² He also that had received two talents came and said, Lord, thou deliveredst unto me two talents: behold, I have gained two other talents beside them.

²³ His lord said unto him, Well done, good and faithful servant; thou hast been faithful over a few things, I will make thee ruler over many things: enter thou into the joy of thy lord.

²⁴ Then he which had received the one talent came and said, Lord, I knew thee that thou art an hard man, reaping where thou hast not sown, and gathering where thou hast not strawed:

²⁵ And I was afraid, and went and hid thy talent in the earth: lo, there thou hast that is thine.

[26] His lord answered and said unto him, Thou wicked and slothful servant, thou knewest that I reap where I sowed not, and gather where I have not strawed:

So I say again don't bury your talent, if you have done so dig it up. It's time to take action.

Let me share with you my testimony on how I got started, before I started my business I worked at Wal-Mart in the day and Blockbuster at night, I hated every minute of it. The only thing I liked about it was that they cut the checks on time. It was a definite paycheck every two weeks.

I was a slave to their company. They controlled my Destiny. They told me what to do and when to do it, when I could eat, when I could have off, and if I could go to my son's basketball and football games. Thank God, now that I am the CEO of my own company, I can do pretty much anything I want.

This all started when I got the idea that on Sunday evenings after me and my family went to church and had Sunday dinner; we would start a new tradition to go to the bookstore to buy books or magazines.

One Sunday me and my family were in "Books A Million," and I saw a magazine sticking up out of the magazine rack and it said, "Web Made Millionaire" and it struck my eye so I began skimming through it and reading it. What I was reading was so electrifying, it captivated me; I immediately decided I wanted to quit Wal-Mart & Blockbuster and start my own business from home. But things don't always happen quite as fast as we want; sometimes we have to build our faith up to get to the point where God wants us.

So what I did was punk out for another year and didn't step out on my faith and do what God called me to do. One night a year later, I was watching the movie, "The Pursuit of Happyness," if you haven't seen it Will Smith played a guy named Chris Gardner and told his story of how he struggled to provide for his family, to the point where he and his son ended up homeless. By the end of the movie Chris Gardner got the job he worked so hard to get, after I saw everything he went through and all the things he did to reach his goal, I was crying.

I told God that even if I ended up like Chris Gardner and had to sleep in a bathroom stall, I was going to trust him,

Step out and do this thing on faith. I made up my mind, I'm going to do it, I'm going to quit.

The next day I went back to work and as soon as I walked in I got called to the office, Wal-Mart told me they were going to send me to Arkansas for a week for what was called a shareholders meeting. I said great, this is going to be a good time to get away, to travel and they were paying for everything. So I said cool of course. I got to Arkansas and got checked into my room.

The next day we had several different events we could choose to attended, so I chose this one particular meeting. I walked in and all of a sudden the real Chris Gardner from the movie The Pursuit of Happyness was walking towards me. Immediately I recognized the spirit of God, he put both of us in the same place at the same time and at that moment I knew I was walking towards my destiny just by that happening. This was not a coincidence, it was truly the hand of God.

(The Picture I Took Of Chris Gardner At The Event In Arkansas)

God showed me where he took Chris from and where he was taking me and at that point in our lives He put us in the same place, so immediately I knew that God was calling me to do my own thing. When I came back home I decided I was going to do it; put in my two weeks' notice.

God said don't do it now, your last day can't be until July 15th and I didn't understand that, but I went ahead and said alright I'm going to wait because God said July 15th. So the next Friday night I'm watching TBN and Bishop Walker III is hosting and he has Bishop Bloomer on. Bishop Bloomer is in the spirit and he's going in and he's saying "the angels of the Lord are here right now, they're right now in your living room doing that thing you want them to do, that thing is done, whatever you're believing God for it is done he said I don't care if its July 15th, that thing is done." So immediately you know what I did I began to get up to praise God, I got up jumping , shouting and praising God so hard, I fell out in the spirit.

You know what was so real and amazing about that experience of what God did, He reached inside me and confirmed His Word to me; He really touched me that night. I will never forget that night. So the next day at work, I put in my notice to quit on July 15th and I told God there was no way I could turn back, after Him revealing that to me in my life. I have never looked back since, I have been building my company ever since making passive income, selling products, developing websites, and helping other people dreams come true by showing them how to provide income using their passion. There was no way I could have told God no, once I asked Him to come on the water and He told me to come.

My personal relationship with God has grown tremendously throughout this whole process. I want to encourage you to trust God, have faith and He can do the same in your life. Don't worry about the circumstances just trust God and keep your eyes on Him. If you begin to sink cry out and ask Him to save you and He will.

HERE IS WHAT YOU NEED TO DO NOW

If you don't do but one income stream you need to release your book.

Everybody has a book in them!

Becoming a Published Author Will Open Up So Many Doors / Opportunities You Probably Never Dreamed Of!

If you have ever wanted to be invited to speak at a conference, workshop etc. A book puts you in line as the expert!

Think about it, not only will you get an honorarium for speaking; you can now go in the lobby and sell your books and put more spending cash in your pocket! Imagine that flight home with an extra $1,000 - $2,000 in your pocket!

I Know You Want More Money!

I Know You Want A Change In Your Life!

I Know You Want A Job where every day Is Payday?

I'm Going to Sell You On Things You Know You Should Be Doing...

I'm Going to Sell You On Taking The Actions You Know You Need To Take!

I'm Going to Sell You On A Whole New Life Of Freedom!

Say These Three Words Below Out Loud!

TAKE ACTION NOW!

Because If Tomorrow Never Comes...

What You Don't Do Today, Doesn't Get Done!

What I'm About to share with you will change your life!

I'm Going to Share With You The Ultimate Publishing Package!

Before I Found My Passion…

I told you I Worked Two Jobs 16-17 hour Days To
Support My Family!

I Used Too…

- Be afraid to lose that job I hated..
- Have to ask to go to my son's football and
  basketball games
- Ask can I have a day off for my Anniversary, to
  take my wife to dinner
- Get in trouble if I took too long on break!

I remember my last day at Wal-mart one of the managers
looked at me and said "You'll be just like the rest of them
you'll be back!" I said no I won't, I thank God because He
has been Faithful!

Wal-mart Does Not Control My Destiny Anymore!

I thank God he has blessed me with an opportunity to help people's dreams come true, which was to become published authors!

This young lady is Jessie Rogers, she is 16 and was born blind. We made her dream of becoming a published author come to pass.

WOW She is 16 & Born Blind and you're still making excuses?

More People We Made Dreams Come True

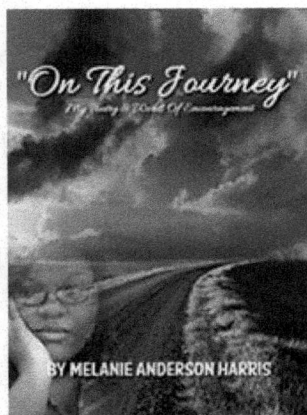

It was always a dream of mine to see a book on the shelf with my name and face on it.

Prime Time Marketing was easy to work with, and took care of everything and at a very reasonable rate!

Thanks again Kelly for everything you did to make another one of my lifetime dreams come true

Melanie Harris
Author of "On This Journey"

With writing my first book, Kelly Cole & Prime Time Marketing have exceeded my expectations.

Kelly's love for what he does pleasantly flowed into every aspect of the publishing process.

His drive and ability to go beyond expectations enforces my desire to work with him and Prime Time Marketing again soon.

Tawana R. Powell
Author of "Life Fulfilled"

Now when I Started My Business, I got invited on a Tele-call....

The guy on the call told me exactly what to do to make my dreams come true.

I Told Him, He Was Crazy!

Guess What?

I didn't **TAKE ACTION**...And It Cost Me At least $50,000!

Yes I achieved some Success, but had I taken action then on what he shared with me, my Success would have come a lot faster!

When I Started To Take Action! I Started Making Money!

Successful People Don't Ask How Much Something Cost, They Ask How Much Will It Make Me!

Question: How Do You Win At Monopoly?

Answer: YOU BUY EVERYTHING!

**I Have A Book Publishing Package Called
The Ultimate Publishing Package!
Completely Turnkey!**

Here Is What It Includes!

We Will Publish your book on Amazon & Amazon Kindle, Barnes & Noble, Books-A-Million & More!

We will complete your book formatting & editing

We will provide you with a unique ISBN #

We will provide an book cover design

We will give physical copies of your book

We will develop a complete marketing plan

We will generate a book trailer/promo video to complement your book and generate interest and sales

Your book will print & ship on-demand, you won't have to touch a thing!

Complete Passive Income!

Plus you will receive a link to order your book wholesale if you would like to have more physical copies to sell in person.

As low as $2.15 per book!

Plus you will maintain all rights to your work & 100% of your profits.

What If I Told You All You Had To Do Was Give Us Your Manuscript?

Your Ultimate Publishing Package

Sets Up Everything For You!

All You Have To Do Is Give Us Your Manuscript!

The Ultimate Publishing Package

- We will Publish your book on Amazon & Amazon Kindle, Barnes & Noble, Books-A-Million & More!
- We will complete your book formatting & editing
- We will provide you with a unique ISBN #
- We will provide an eye-catching book cover
- We will generate physical copies of your book
- We will develop a complete marketing plan
- We will generate a book trailer/promo video to complement your book and generate interest and sales
- Books will print & ship on-demand
- You can order your book wholesale
- You will maintain all rights to your work & 100% of your profits.

Your Ultimate Publishing Package
Sets Up Everything For You!

All You Have To Do Is, Give Us Your Manuscript!

You Can Do THIS!

It's In You!

Here Is What You Need To Do, You Need To Get Signed Up For The Ultimate Publishing Package!

And Get Your Book Published!

It's Your Time To Hold Your Book In Your Hand!

The Ultimate Publishing Package

Get Started Today

www.PublishingAdvantageGroup.com

Limited Time Only!

The Ultimate Publishing Package

We will Publish your book on Amazon & Amazon Kindle, Barnes & Noble, Books-A-Million & More!

We will complete your book formatting & editing

We will provide you with a unique ISBN #

We will provide an appropriate book cover design

We will generate physical copies of your book

We will develop a complete marketing plan

We will generate a book trailer/promo video to complement your book and generate interest and sales

Books will print & ship on-demand

You can order your book wholesale

You maintain all rights to your work & 100% of your profits.

Your Ultimate Publishing Package
Sets Up Everything For You!

All You Have To Do Is, Give Us Your Manuscript!
Get Started Today
www.PublishingAdvantageGroup.com

There Comes a Point in Your Life When You Know You
Need to Take A New Action

**There comes a Point when the thing You Need to do
is Obvious…**

Years from Now You're Going to Look Back at this
Moment, You're going to say he gave me the Opportunity
To Change my Life!

Take Action Now!
Get Signed Up Now Go To:
www.PublishingAdvantageGroup.com

ABOUT THE AUTHOR

Mr. Kelly Cole is CEO of Publishing Advantage Group, 2X #1 Best Selling Author, Book Publisher, Coach & a Speaker. Kelly has been seen on NBC, FOX, ABC, The CW, Gospel Updates Magazine & more. As a consultant, Kelly has worked with clients who have appeared on **OWN, Real House Wives of ATL, Bravo, NBA, WORD network, MTV, BET, Atlantic Records, and more.** Kelly started Publishing Advantage Group 12 Years ago after quitting his day job at Wal-Mart. He almost ended up homeless but worked hard serving and helping other people dreams come true, which ultimately led to his dream coming true of building a successful marketing & publishing company. In 2014, he was elected into the GrindMoves Hall of Fame. He is labeled A Business Guru for his knowledge and marketing wisdom that he has used to help people all over the world! He is the proud father of three: 1 Boy & 2 Girls.

Be Sure And Order The Home Study Course Now!

Includes 2 CD Trainings & 1 DVD Training
www.SolomonWealthFormula.com

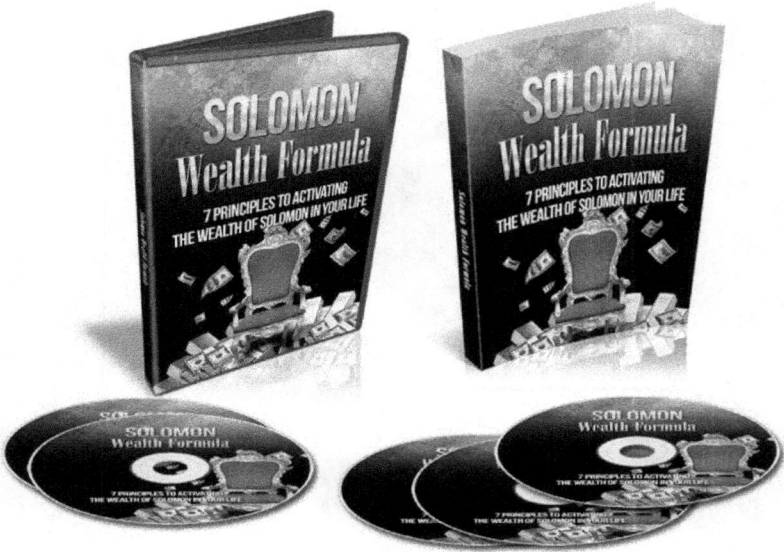

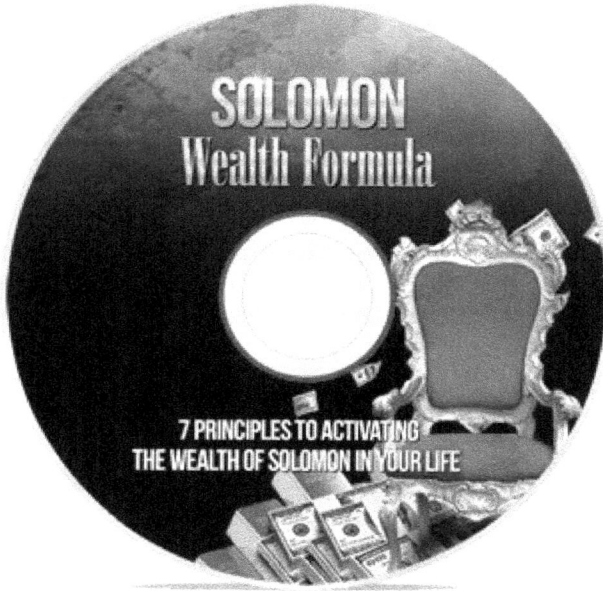

FREE BONUS
Solomon Wealth Formula Audio Training

Be Sure And Download The Audio Training Of
This Book FREE Here:
http://www.SolomonWealthFormula.com/FreeGift

Bonus Chapter

Abundance Programing Affirmations

The Following Statements Are Biblical Affirmations

The Purpose Is To Program Your Mind To Say What God Says and Increase Your Faith By Hearing The Word Repeated to Yourself.

Say the following statements out loud.

I am a follower of Christ

I believe His Word

I am a child of the King

There is no lack in the Kingdom

I have more than enough

I believe in Prosperity

My finances are getting better everyday

I am Blessed

My Family is blessed

The Lord has given me the power to get Wealth

He wants me Wealthy

He wants me Happy

He wants me Healthy

I am the Head and not the Tail

I am the lender and not the borrower

I am above and not beneath

I am a good steward over what God has given me

Wealth is Good

Money is Good

In my Father's house are many Mansions

A cattle on thousand hills belong to my Father

I am Royalty

I Love the Lord

He always provides

I Love to Give

I Am a Tither, That's why I'm blessed

I am a cheerful giver

Abundance is attracted to me

I can have whatever I declare

Life is in my tongue

I have now faith

I am an Unstoppable human being

I easily create great wealth

I am a money magnet

Money is a good thing

Good things always happen to me

I have favor on my life

I love my life

I'm having more fun than I ever have

When I give it comes back to me 100 fold

I refuse to participate in any recession

The Kingdom economy is always good

I deserve the finer things in life

I deserve great abundance

I deserve great joy

I deserve to live life fully

I finish what I start

I am persistent

I am creative

I am totally loved

I am a Victor and not a Victim

God Said It I believe it!

Amen

Speak These Words Over Your Life Every day!

www.ingramcontent.com/pod-product-compliance
Lightning Source LLC
Chambersburg PA
CBHW071115210326
41519CB00020B/6302